Wolf Hill

Fair Scare

D1138361

Roderick Hunt

Illustrated by Alex Brychta

OXFORD
UNIVERSITY PRESS

OXFORD
UNIVERSITY PRESS

Great Clarendon Street, Oxford OX2 6DP

Oxford University Press is a department of the University of Oxford.
It furthers the University's objective of excellence in research, scholarship,
and education by publishing worldwide in

Oxford   New York

Auckland   Cape Town   Dar es Salaam   Hong Kong   Karachi
Kuala Lumpur   Madrid   Melbourne   Mexico City   Nairobi
New Delhi   Shanghai   Taipei   Toronto

With offices in

Argentina   Austria   Brazil   Chile   Czech Republic   France   Greece
Guatemala   Hungary   Italy   Japan   Poland   Portugal   Singapore
South Korea   Switzerland   Thailand   Turkey   Ukraine   Vietnam

Oxford is a registered trade mark of Oxford University Press
in the UK and in certain other countries

Text © Roderick Hunt 2002
Illustrations © Alex Brychta 2002

The moral rights of the author have been asserted

Database right Oxford University Press (maker)

First published 2002

British Library Cataloguing in Publication Data

Data available

ISBN 978-0-19-919524-4

Chapter 1

Najma's dad was washing his car.

'If you want to help,' he said, 'you can give it a polish and clean the inside.'

'Do I have to?' asked Najma.

'Extra pocket money?' said Mr Patel.

'All right then,' laughed Najma.

Najma was glad to earn some money. The fair was coming to Wolf Hill and she wanted to go.

She was polishing the car when Loz came round to play.

'I need the extra money,' said Najma. 'The rides at the fair are so expensive.'

Loz sighed. She lived with her grandmother. She knew Nan couldn't afford to give her money to go to the fair.

Then Loz had an idea. Maybe there was a way to *earn* some money to spend at the fair.

Chapter 2

That afternoon Loz and Najma walked down Wolf Street. They had a bucket and some sponges.

They called at several houses, but no one was in.

At last they saw a man outside his house painting his window.

'Do you want your car cleaning?' asked Loz. 'We don't charge a lot.'

'Well, all right,' said the man. 'But don't scratch the paint work.'

Najma and Loz set to work. Then Mr Patel drove past in his car. He stopped when he saw the girls.

'You must never call at strange houses,' he said, crossly. 'Stop what you are doing and say sorry to the man.'

Loz was upset. Her idea had got Najma into trouble, and she still had no money to go to the fair.

Chapter 3

Every year the fair came to Wolf Hill on the first Monday and Tuesday in October. It was set up in Market Street, which was closed to traffic.

At school on Monday everyone was excited. Most of them were going to the fair that evening.

'My brother's taking Gizmo and me,' said Chris.

Najma said she was going with her dad.

Loz didn't say anything. She knew Nan would never take her.

9

Then Najma turned to Loz and said, 'Do you want to come with us?'

'I'd have to ask Nan,' said Loz. She hoped that Nan would say no. She had no money to spend, even if she did go.

Chapter 4

That evening Loz went to the fair with Najma. Nan said she could go. Then Loz had a surprise – a big one! Nan had given her some money to spend.

Najma and Loz could hear the
fair long before they got there. They
began to walk more and more quickly.

'Slow down, you two,' said Mr Patel.
'I can't keep up with you.'

It was starting to get dark when they
got to Market Street.

12

The fair looked bright and dazzling.
The stalls were lit up and the rides
had hundreds of brightly-coloured
flashing bulbs.

They could smell hot dogs and
candy floss.

Most of the big rides were expensive and it cost a lot to have a go on a stall.

'I have enough money for one ride and two goes to win a soft toy,' said Loz.

'Well, let's look at the fair, first,' said Mr Patel. 'Then you can both decide what to go on.'

FARE
£2
EACH PERSON
50p TO VIEW

Chapter 5

They met Chris and Gizmo. Najma asked if they could all go off together.

Mr Patel said they could. 'But I want you girls back here in half an hour,' he said. 'Don't be late.'

They watched a ride called The Moon Force. It was like a huge drum.

People stood inside. The drum began to spin. Then the floor dropped away. People stuck to the wall.

'You wouldn't get me on that!' said Chris. 'It turns you upside down.'

Loz wasn't sure if she wanted to go on any of the rides. They all looked far too scary.

Chapter 6

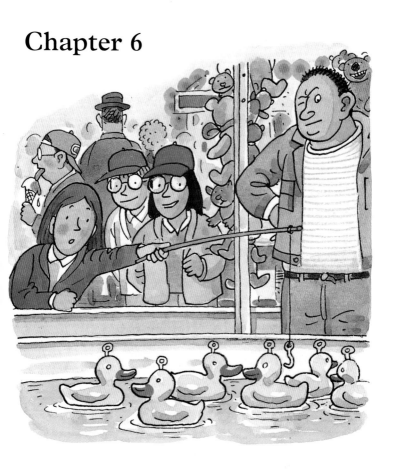

Loz liked the prizes on a stall where you had to hook a duck on the end of a rod. She decided to try. Hooking the duck was easy. Loz chose a small teddy bear as her prize.

They all decided it was time to have a ride.

Chris and Gizmo wanted to go on the dodgem cars. They didn't want to share a car. They both wanted to drive.

In the end, Najma went in Chris's car and Loz went in Gizmo's.

At first the dodgem cars were fun. Then they kept being hit by other cars.

Gizmo's car got locked into a big jam. It took a long time to get going again.

Loz had shared the cost of the ride with Gizmo. She didn't have much money left.

Chapter 7

They came to a big wheel. It had cages that swung backwards and forwards when the wheel went round.

'I can afford one more ride,' said Gizmo. 'Let's go on that. I bet you can see over Wolf Hill from the top of it.'

Loz said she couldn't go on the wheel. 'I don't have enough money,' she said.

Najma looked in her purse. 'Well, I'll pay for you,' she said. 'Come on.'

So Loz and Chris got into the last cage and the ride began.

Loz found the ride exciting. The cage swung forwards as they went over the top. It felt very high up.

As they came down, the cage swung backwards. Loz laughed. 'This is scary but fun,' she thought.

Chris gripped the bar that held them in. 'Sit still, Loz,' he shouted. 'Don't rock the cage.'

Loz could see that he was terrified. His eyes were closed and he pressed himself back into the seat. His arms were rigid and his face looked white.

'I'm going to be sick,' he said.

Then there was a loud crunching and grinding sound. The cage rocked wildly. The wheel stopped with a jolt. People screamed.

Chapter 8

The wheel had broken down. The cage rocked gently, then hung still. Everyone on the wheel was stuck. Chris and Loz were stuck at the top.

Loz felt scared, but she was sure they would soon fix the wheel. She looked at Chris. He was shaking with fright. His eyes were tightly shut and his body was stiff.

She leaned forward and put her hand on his arm. The cage rocked with the movement.

'Please don't move,' gasped Chris. 'Just keep still, Loz.'

Loz looked down. Below her two men were mending a broken pulley.

In the crowd she could see Mr Patel, but she didn't dare wave. She didn't want to rock the cage.

Chapter 9

Loz and Chris were stuck for ages.

Then the wheel began to move slowly.

It started and stopped in a series of jerks. Chris moaned. 'Why can't they just get us down?' he said.

Loz knew she had to take Chris's
mind off his fears. She began to talk
to him. She talked about school. She
talked about television programmes
and pop music.

Slowly the cage moved downwards. At last they were on the ground, and they both got out.

Chris's face still looked pale. 'Well done, Chris,' whispered Loz. 'You found out you're scared of heights, but I thought you were very brave.'

'Thanks, Loz,' replied Chris. 'I'm glad it was you who was with me.'

They found Najma and Gizmo.

'That was terrible,' said Najma. 'I won't go on a big wheel again in a hurry.'

Chapter 10

One good thing happened. Mr Patel complained and everyone on the ride got double their money back.

Loz was able to repay Najma for the ride.

'We've got enough for another go on something,' said Gizmo.

'No thank you,' said Loz. 'I'm not sure I like fairground rides very much.'

Mr Patel grinned. 'Well you must have had a wonderful view of Wolf Hill from the top of the wheel.'

Loz smiled at Chris. 'A wonderful view? It was all so scary, we forgot to look,' she said.